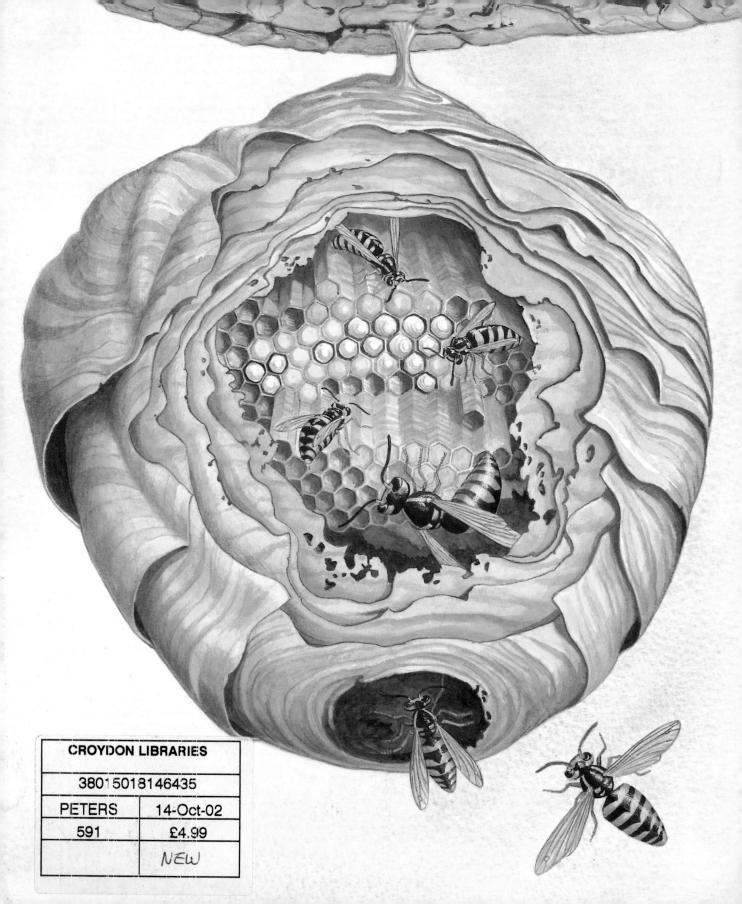

Cycles of Life

Animal Builders

Written by David Stewart
Illustrated by Sean Milne
Created and designed by David Salariya

BOOK HOUSE

Contents

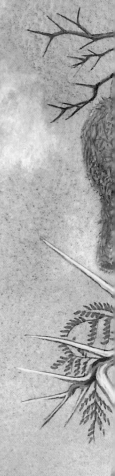

Introduction

Animals build shelters to protect themselves from the heat, the cold, rain, snow or wind. Their shelters also give them a safe and warm place to bring up their babies.

Animals make different kinds of shelters. The type of shelter they build depends on where they live and what materials they can find to use.

In this book you will see how five different animals make different kinds of shelters.

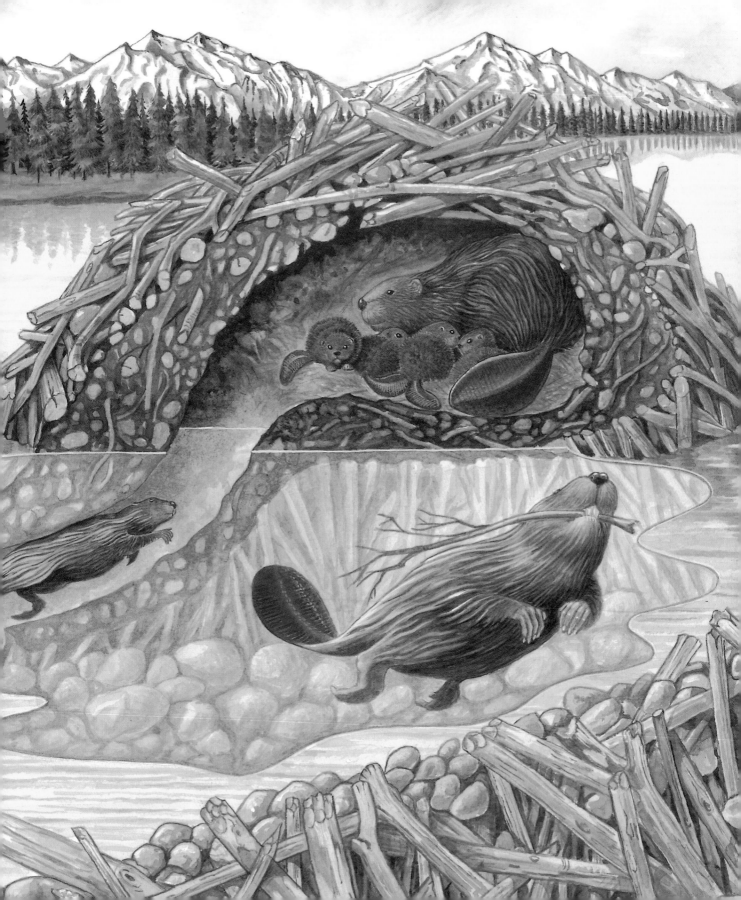

The wasp nest

Wasps are insects.
They live in a big family
group inside the nest.

In spring, a female wasp
called a queen builds a nest
from wood pulp. Inside the
nest she builds a comb,
made up of many cells.
She lays eggs in these
cells. Wasps, called
workers, hatch
from the eggs.

Workers

Nest

The queen chews dry wood to make it into wood pulp.

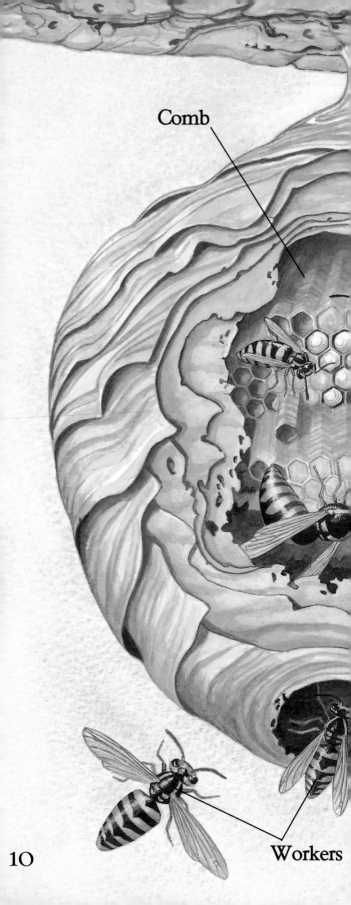

Comb

Workers

10

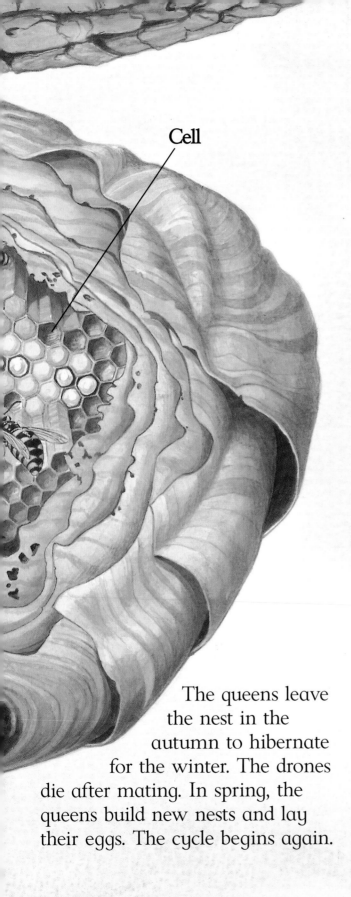

Cell

Once the workers have hatched, they take over building the cells that make up the nest.

Towards the end of summer, the queen lays larger eggs. These eggs contain new queens. She also lays eggs which contain male wasps, called drones. The drones and the new queens mate.

The queens leave the nest in the autumn to hibernate for the winter. The drones die after mating. In spring, the queens build new nests and lay their eggs. The cycle begins again.

The weaver bird nest

These birds are called weaver birds because their nests look like they are woven.

In fact, the birds use their beaks and feet to loop, twist and knot strips of leaves and grass.

Weaver bird

Young birds often make messy nests. As the birds get more practice, their nests become neater and stronger.

Snake

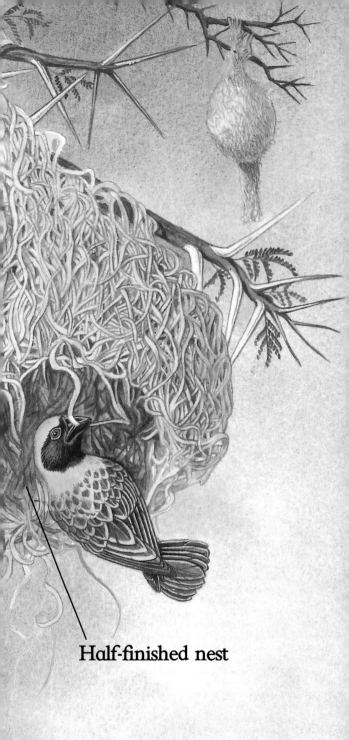

Half-finished nest

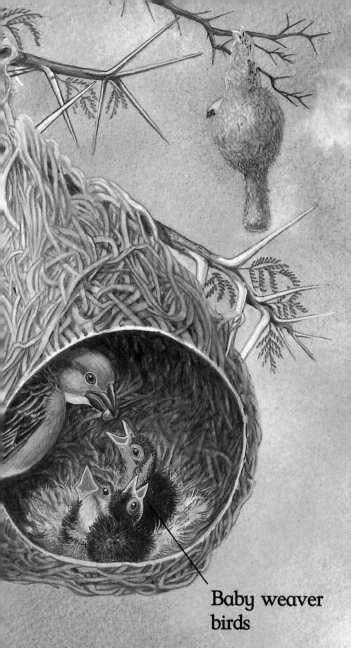

The male bird builds the nest. If a female thinks it's good enough, she lines it with feathers and lays her eggs.

The special hanging shape of the nest protects the eggs and baby birds from snakes and lizards.

Baby weaver birds

The parents feed the baby birds with seed. When the baby birds are old enough they fly and find their own food.

The woodpecker nest

Woodpeckers like to live
near trees. These can be
in woods or in gardens.

A woodpecker pecks a
hole in a tree trunk with
its strong beak to make
its nest.

The woodpecker also
uses its beak to tap tree
trunks in search of
insects to eat.

Squirrel

16

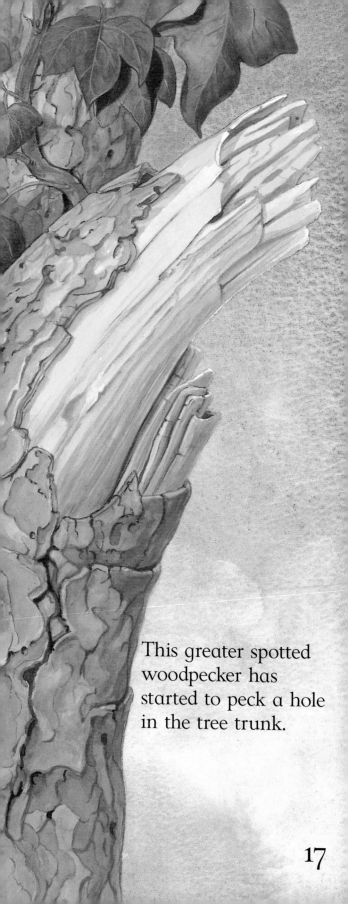

This greater spotted
woodpecker has
started to peck a hole
in the tree trunk.

The female woodpecker lays between four and seven white eggs inside the hole in the tree trunk.

The eggs hatch after 16 days. The baby birds are able to fly three weeks later.

The male and the female woodpecker take it in turns to sit on the eggs in the nest and keep them warm.

Baby woodpeckers

The beaver lodge

Beavers are mammals.
They live and work in
small family groups.
After mating, the male
and female beavers stay
together all their lives.
They both help to build
their home which is
called a lodge.

Lodge made
from sticks
and mud

Beavers chew through tree
branches with their huge
razor-sharp teeth. These
teeth grow as fast as they
are worn down.

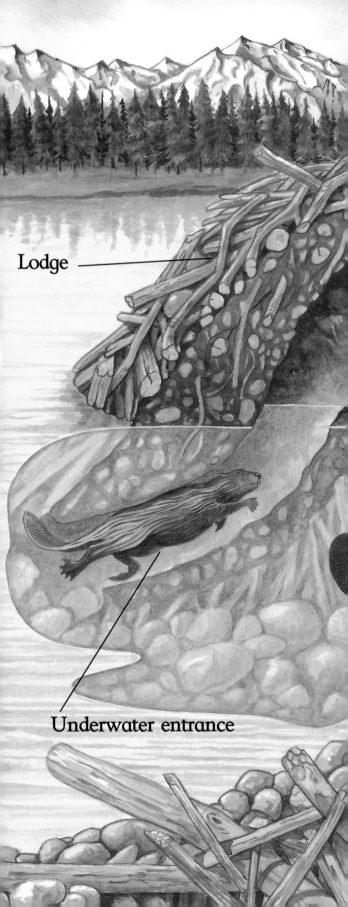

Lodge

Underwater entrance

The beavers live inside the lodge, which is called a chamber. This is above the water level.

They also build a dam near by. This floods the area around the lodge. The entrance tunnel to the lodge can then be kept under water so that the young beavers are protected from other animals.

Baby beavers

Chamber

Dam

The badger sett

Badgers are mammals. They usually live in woodlands.

Badgers dig their homes under the ground. These are called setts. Each sett has at least two entrances and many tunnels and chambers.

Badgers will eat almost anything, including earthworms, mice, voles, frogs, snails and wasps.

Entrance to sett

Badger cub

Badgers keep their setts very clean.

Badgers keep their
setts very clean.

Badgers sleep during the day and go out to look for food at night. This is why they are usually seen early in the morning or late at night.

Badger babies are called cubs. One to five cubs are born, usually in February. The cubs will remain with their parents until the autumn.

27

Animal builders

All of these animals have built completely different types of shelters using different materials and building techniques.

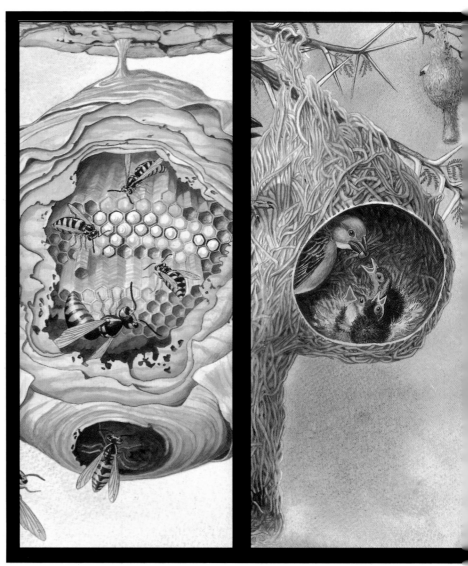

Paper maker
The wasps' nest is made from a papery material. The wasps make this by mixing chewed wood with saliva.

Weaver
The weaver birds' nest is made from pieces of grass which the birds knot and twist together.

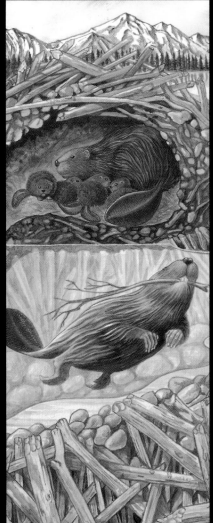

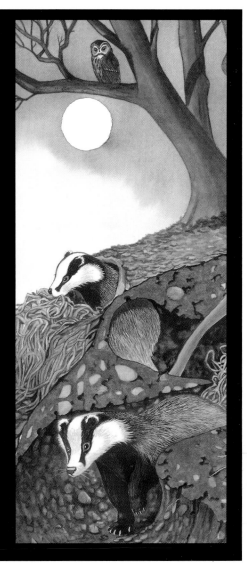

Driller
The woodpeckers build their nest by pecking a hole in the trunk of a tree using their beaks.

Dam builder
The beavers' lodge is made from sticks and mud. They also build a dam to flood the area around their lodge.

Burrower
Badgers build their setts underground by burrowing through the earth.

29

Animal builder words

Beak
The hard and pointed part around the mouth of a bird.

Cell
Parts of a wasps' nest in which eggs are laid and hatched. Each cell has eight sides and is made from paper.

Chamber
The living area of shelters made by animals such as beavers and badgers.

Comb
A group of many cells that all fit together inside a wasps' nest.

Dam
A type of wall built by beavers across a lake or river. Dams are made from sticks and they stop the water flowing away.

Drones
Fertile male wasps; they mate with the queen wasps before dying in the autumn.

Hibernate
When animals spend the winter months sleeping for weeks on end in a nest or shelter.

Insect
An animal that has a hard outer covering and a body divided into three parts. Insects have six legs.

Lodge
The house that beavers build to live in. It is made from sticks and mud.

Mammal
A warm-blooded animal, usually with fur or hair.

Mate
When a male and female join together to have babies.

Queen wasp
The largest wasp in the nest, whose main job is to lay eggs. She is the mother of all the other wasps in the nest.

Saliva
A clear liquid in the mouth which helps animals chew and swallow food. Wasps use saliva to help them chew wood into a soft pulp.

Worker wasp
Female wasps that cannot lay eggs. Their main job is to feed the grubs in the nest, help build the nest and look after the queen.

Index

Language Consultant:
Betty Root

Natural History Consultant:
Dr Gerald Legg

Editors:
Stephanie Cole
Karen Barker Smith

Published in Great Britain in 2002 by
Book House, an imprint of
The Salariya Book Company Ltd
Book House, 25 Marlborough Place,
Brighton BN1 1UB

Visit the Salariya Book Company at:
www.salariya.com
www.book-house.co.uk

A catalogue record for this book is
available from the British Library.

ISBN 1 904194 27 3

Printed and bound in China.

Printed on paper from sustainable forests.